LAST WORDS
To a
DYING HEART

MANUEL V. JOHNSON

LAST WORDS TO A DYING HEART

Copyright © 2015 - Manuel V. Johnson

Published in the United States
Manuel V. Johnson

ISBN-10: 0-9861430-2-2
ISBN-13: 978-0-9861430-2-1

For More Info:

Printed in the United States of America

About this book

This collection features one hundred original quotes created to inspire, encourage, guide, and give a voice to the emotions many people struggle to express. Each quote is followed by a brief reflection that expands on its meaning. Some messages speak for themselves, while others may require a deeper look. At times, you may notice a theme repeated in different ways - this is intentional, because certain truths deserve emphasis.

If there's anything you read here that you'd like clarity on - or if something in your personal life or relationship feels heavy, confusing, or uncertain - I invite you to reach out:

My hope for this book is simple:
If even one person closes these pages seeing life, love, or themselves in a new light… then this work has done what it was created to do.

Thank you for reading.
Your time, your trust, and your openness mean more than you know.

- Manuel V. Johnson

LAST WORDS
To a
DYING HEART

<u>**The Discovery**</u>

It lay there on the cold floor, bleeding out its last bit of
life. I picked it up and held it in my hands, rubbing it
gently with my thumbs, doing everything I could to keep
it steady. It shook and trembled from the lack of love it
had received.

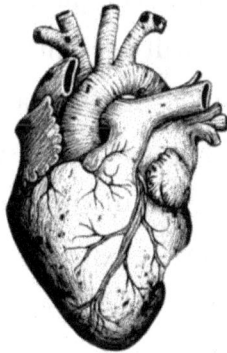

ASK DR. LINQ

"I've been through so much, but I face the world fearless. I've cried and I've hurt, but now I carry on tearless."

We all go through some type of disappointment in life. I've always found comfort in knowing that these low points are lessons. You always have to try to learn something from those times in your life. In order to get to **Stage 2**, you have to learn from **Stage 1**. Every new stage will present a new challenge; be ready. These perceived failures are merely tools for you to better build your future with. Once you've gained from this low point, you're even more prepared for your next challenge. But now that you know how it works, you'll be mentally aware of what's happening. You can't win a war that you don't know you're fighting.

"Don't push me away with your actions and ask me to stay with your words. Don't love me with all your heart and hate me to death with your thoughts. Don't rub my back with your hands and then stab it with my trust. Don't say you're ready to start, then be the reason we're falling apart."

It almost seems unfair that someone can be so two faced. All you ask is that they don't waste your time. But sometimes they themselves don't realize it. That occasionally happens when you meet people who always go with the flow and never have a direct goal. They sometimes lose track of what they're doing because they're on autopilot, not realizing that their actions are affecting the person they once said they love: you.

ASK DR. LINQ

"You can't be available for those you aren't obligated to be available for and then get upset when they start to take you for granted."

Sometimes we have to limit the amount of time we give people; not everyone is worthy of our attention. Especially those who aren't helping us succeed in life. Those who hold us back and keep us in stressful moods are the ones we should try our hardest to separate from. Unfortunately, sometimes those are the ones we fall in love with, and that's when we're faced with a hard decision. Naturally, when in love, you would normally like to put that person's feelings before yours in hopes that they'd do the same for you. But when that person has shown you they aren't willing to put your feelings first, it may be wise to return the favor. And if you decide not to, remember it was your choice.

"Today is a good day to delete some people who aren't positive in your life."

When is a great time to delete negative people? The answer is always "right now." There's never *not* a good time. You have one life to live, and I suggest you live it as positively as possible. The environment around you can affect the results of your life. If you hang with people who aren't trying to progress, chances are you won't either. Am I saying it's guaranteed that you can't grow in life around negative people? No, there's no guarantee. But I can assure you that your chances will increase tremendously when you associate yourself with the type of people you want to become.

"I forgot to tell myself I'm sorry for all the times I treated myself less than what I am. For that, I will forever be in debt to myself."

I apologize. We have to treat ourselves like we're one of a kind. Why? Because we are! We waste so much time and so much of our potential on nonsensical things: items, people, and activities. We have to make a change; before we can, we have to first recognize the problem and apologize to ourselves. Then make a promise that we will spend the rest of our life making it right. I'm not suggesting that we should live with a burden of regret, but at the moment of apology we should replace our old habits with new ones. That way the promise we made comes naturally and is not carried on our back as a burden.

"I didn't cry because you hurt me, I cried because I lowered my standards for you."

When you put someone first and they spit in your face, it's almost like the ultimate low blow. But what's worse is when you sacrifice who you are as a person for them, and they still cause sorrow in your life. I always recommend finding someone who fits the person you are instead of being molded into someone you're not, unless that new mold is an improvement from the type of person you currently are. If they cause you to raise your standards and it doesn't work out between you two, you still gained something good. If they allow you to keep your standards where they are and it doesn't work out, you lost nothing. But if they cause you to lower your standards and it doesn't work, it not only hurts, but it scars your inner self deeply.

"Sex is good, but mental sex is better."

It's not often you meet someone who can stimulate your body and mind. But when you do, it can be something so special. A person who can make you see something in yourself that you didn't see before you met them – that's the type of person you should be involved with. When curiosity is fed, it smiles through the heart. So feast up and love more.

"You've looked in the mirror over 5,000 times and you've found every flaw. Not realizing how beautiful you are through someone else's eyes."

Sometimes we're our own worst critics. It's good to check ourselves before the world does, but it's also good to remember that we are all perfect. None of us are meant to be alike and none of us are meant to be without flaws. Our perceived flaws are the building blocks for self-improvement. Being that self-improvement and growth are natural, it's perfect. We are meant to grow from where we once were. So embrace those flaws, and don't let them get you down. Some of the prettiest people in the world suffer from this, and it's sad. When you begin to live a positive life, you literally start to see yourself differently. The funny part is that other people often don't notice these flaws. It's in your mind and in how you personally perceive yourself. Have you ever had someone tell you how beautiful you looked and you didn't believe them? This may be about you then.

"The older I get the more I find myself talking to myself. I'm starting to think I'm the only one I can trust."

It seems that with time we shed those who aren't a part of our next journey. They were perfect for where we were, even if they may have caused us pain - it was much needed oddly enough. Moving forward, their services are no longer needed; their role in this movie called *"My Life"* isn't as big as it once was. I'm not sad about who's gone, I'm too busy being excited about who's coming into my life next.

ASK DR. LINQ

"When it goes bad, don't fight it - it's apart of the process. When it rains, we don't try to stop it; we shelter from it and wait for the sun."

Easier said than done, I know, but what isn't? Look, you can't spend your precious time "fighting," spend it "loving." When someone tries to force you into a fight, try to avoid it. I've learned that conversations about serious issues are important, but once those turn into mud-slinging fights, it's time to go under my "positive umbrella" for shelter. Without the bad, we can't appreciate the good. The longer you fight it, the longer it stays around. The faster you let it do what it's there to do, the faster it will leave. Then you can spend that free time building a bigger umbrella.

"The only reason I burn bridges is to keep you from following me across it."

Those of your past are in the past for a reason. Oftentimes there's no reason to look back and no reason to allow them back into your life. Sometimes we get comfy with people and develop strong connections that we think are meant to stay connected. But often those connections are meant to be severed. They're severed not only because you shouldn't go back to them, but occasionally it's to keep them from trying to reach you.

"Make everyone that has you - afraid to lose you. Be the unique person you're supposed to be; don't be everyone else. Clones can't be special."

Standing out from the crowd is the best way to make yourself memorable. If you bring the same thing to the table as the ones who came before you, you just may be put in the same category as them. Add value to your life, not for anyone else's benefit, but for your own. Make your life one of value, that way you can raise the value bar of the kind of person you expect to have. You can't bring 3 to the table and expect someone to bring 20, you have to at least bring 16. So raise your value, become the 20, and make them tremble at the idea of losing you. There are too many people who don't even value their own lives but are waiting for someone to see the value in it.

"The day you stop trying to make your ex regret the breakup, is the day you've finally moved on."

Until that day comes, whether you realize it or not, your actions may still be slightly affected by their existence, knowing that their eyes may be on you. When you reach that point when you really couldn't care less, you know it's officially behind you. Besides, the best way for you to progress forward is to let go of those things that are behind you. You can't steal home plate and keep your foot on 3rd base. It can be a beautiful moment when you're no longer bothered by their games because you're too busy being excited about the person you're becoming. Worrying about them is just adding unnecessary thought to your already busy mind. You can use the breakup itself for motivation moving forward, but once that's complete, it's home sweet home.

"You have to wash away the failures of filth from your previous relationship, with the waters of new wisdom you've gained from it."

Those things that seem to be worthless missions can be months or even years in detention. But once that time has ceased, your heart will be released and it's back to school as usual. You may be bitter about how it ended, but I'm sure you've learned a valuable lesson at some point while in it. That seemingly small lesson is probably the entire purpose of the relationship in the first place. So don't view the glass as half empty, see it as half full and understand that you are a stronger person for making it through such a hard time.

"Nothing is wrong with them not viewing marriage as an ultimate goal - that's fine. The problem comes when they commit to someone who does place marriage as a goal."

Nothing is wrong with them choosing to be single. It becomes an issue when that decision is made while in a relationship, especially when they don't inform their partner about it until they're caught being *single*. This is why I often tell women to make sure you tell the person you're dealing with your intentions and do not be afraid to scare guys away. If you scare him away, that just means he wasn't for you. You may have dodged a bullet.

<u>The Examination</u>

.... It was as cold as the hard floor from which I found it. I wonder how it got here. More importantly, why was it left here. I turned it over and saw a bandage on the back. I could tell that it's been broken before; so delicate to the touch...

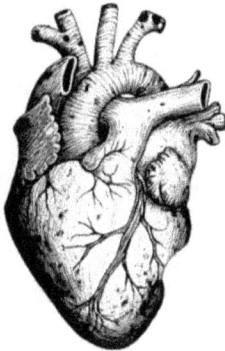

"When you're such an honest person, it's kind of hard to accept the idea of someone lying while looking you in the eyes - but it happens."

Sometimes we place people so high on a pedestal that when we find out they're not worthy to be there, we vow to never repeat that action again. Sometimes when you take pride in being an honest person, you may find yourself placing others who you love in this honesty box with you. We all expect to get back what we give in most cases, but it doesn't always work out that way. What we have to understand is that believing in others is a risk; giving your heart to someone is a risk. We never truly know how people will handle these things we give them. But what we can do is say to ourselves now:

- I love myself unconditionally.
- I held up my end of the bargain.
- I will be just fine moving forward.

Their ill wills are theirs; everyone has their own evils to deal with at some point. Don't allow those evils to affect you too. Not always easy but must be understood.

ASK DR. LINQ

"You two have just broken up. So before you get on social media and start acting out of character...I just want to tell you that you're beautiful and you'll be just fine. Continue to be the self-respecting person you say you are."

Sometimes we try to do too much so that the world can see we're okay. But sometimes it can look so insincere; just relax and be your normal self. Before you call that one close friend, before you start posting sexual pictures and posts to draw attention online, remember that a breakup doesn't require you to act over the top. Never cater to the thoughts of others, especially if it's at the expense of your dignity.

"Don't stress over things that you can't control."

No matter how logical this sounds, we often forget this simple rule. Why? Maybe we can't imagine being powerless over situations we want to be in control of. That's understandable, but we have to wake up and smell the roses. If it's stressing us, we either have to put ourselves in a position to call the shots or leave it alone. The key word in this is stress. Stress can subtract years off your life; is it worth that?

"After a while you start to wonder why you are fighting for someone who is clearly fighting against you."

When you find yourself in a situation where you feel you are fighting to make something work, make sure the person you are trying to make it work with is not fighting against you. More often than not, I hear women in particular say that they are fighting for their relationship to work. When I ask who is giving them problems and they tell me their significant other is, I smile and tell them that is who they are fighting against, their significant other. Sometimes people have a hard time accepting this simple truth. The fact of the matter is, it is hard to win a boxing match when the person who is in your corner cheering you on is the same person across from you in the ring. Ding-Ding.

"No matter how relaxing your vacation spot is, you'll never rest if your stress travels with you."

The mind is a terrible thing to waste. It is also a terrible thing to fill with waste. Some time away can definitely help with the emptying of the mind, a lot of laughter as well and even meditation. But if you are on this trip still speaking about the very things you are trying to escape, there is no point. Keep in mind that a vacation does not make problems disappear in most cases. A vacation is merely a timeout for you to step back and tackle your problems with a clear mind. The beautiful part of having a clear mind is that you will be on a permanent vacation and it is a lot cheaper. The goal is to make everyday life feel like a resort getaway.

"Even though you're what I want, you're not what I need."

You may have to save yourself from yourself. Our desires can be so strong that we will choose things we know we should not have, just for useless pleasures. We also prefer fun over education and fruits over vegetables. Keep in mind, both are good, but the key word is **both**. It is good to want the person you need, and that is a beautiful thing. It is also good when you recognize the wrong in the person you wanted and can make changes before they completely hurt you.

ASK DR. LINQ

"The older I get, the pickier I become; maybe I just know what I want and I expect it now."

It feels like with age we tend to get to a point where we no longer take on senseless relationships or friendships. As we get up in age, we've seen so much that we can smell it coming from a mile away. A situation in the past that you may have entertained before doesn't seem worth entertaining anymore. I know what I want and need, and I can't settle for anything less than that. When you spend the majority of your life building value, it's only right you get a return on your investment.

ASK DR. LINQ

"If you don't want me, then I don't want you; I'll keep telling that lie, until it comes true."

Sometimes we have to speak things into existence; it's part of Universal Law. When dealing with a breakup, we often go through rough patches where we deeply miss the other person. In order to get ourselves back on the road, we occasionally have to give ourselves a jump start. This beautiful lie is that jump start. We tell ourselves this lie until it becomes our reality. Keep in mind, this works with any seed you plant in your head. So make sure you plant some good ones in there and watch them grow!

"They've hurt you and you want to make sure they feel what you felt. Don't waste your time; you may not be able to hurt a cold heart - move on."

The revenge is to do better without them, to elevate your life. Not spend time looking back. If you worry about them, they've won. You win by becoming the best you that you can be, keep it pushing. If they're a cold-hearted individual, you probably won't be able to do much damage. Just let hell freeze over. When they see that you've progressed without them, it'll cut them deep. One day it won't matter either way.

ASK DR. LINQ

"Doesn't matter what qualities you show if the person you're showing them to doesn't know the value."

You can be the best person on earth. But if the person you choose to show this greatness to isn't aware of what greatness is, they will take it for granted. Don't get mad at them; just understand that they probably weren't on your level yet. You might want to pick your fruit from higher up on the tree next time.

"It's funny how walking down the wrong road can take you to the right destination."

Life works that way sometimes. It kind of makes you question what exactly is "wrong." What if there is no wrong, and what if everything we perceive as wrong is merely a lesson on the path to success? Instead, our success is determined by how well we take that lesson and use it. Occasionally, you can be heading in the opposite direction of what you intended and end up somewhere even better. If you're always looking for the good in life, it will find you. If you look for the bad, it will too.

"Sometimes you have to give people what they ask for. Just to show them that's not what they really wanted."

When people get ahead of themselves, sometimes you have to pull their chain and help them slow down. They ask for space in a relationship, okay, give it to them. They want to erase the space; keep the space there. They have to understand that they can't just come and go as they please. If you two are a team, you make decisions as a team unless they want to jump ship. But let them know that since they've switched ships, your ship is now lighter and a little faster; you may not be there when they try to jump aboard.

"Never kill who you are while waiting to see who he is."

If you have to forget what you stand for just to play the waiting game, I don't feel it's worth the trade. If what you stand for doesn't align with the person you're trying to get to know, then they aren't someone you should be trying to get to know. Align yourself with like-minded people, positive people, and grow. Getting out of character is only good when your original character is bad. On the flip side of the coin, sometimes we can see that a particular person isn't any good for us, but we continue to entertain their presence. Most of the time it's because we see something in them that they haven't discovered themselves, so we are waiting for them to find it. But in the process of waiting for them, don't forget who you are.

"You can kiss me 100 times and then spit on me once; that one time will wash away every kiss."

It can take years to build our foundation and only minutes to make it crumble. Sometimes their actions are so terrible you have no choice but to let the wrecking ball crash the walls. You two can always build it again if it's still worth it. So if there is a next time, they know better. But if you don't feel the want or need to rebuild, don't. You'll just be wasting their time and, more importantly, your own. There's no need to drag out the process.

"Your anger should cost so much that only a few can afford it."

Let's try not to make it so affordable that any stranger can come along and have access to it. It's worth so much because it takes so much from you. Being upset normally doesn't change people on the outside of us; it normally changes the person on the inside of us. It's a process though; continue to work on it.

The Diagnosis

... I removed the bandage and noticed it had been cut pretty deep. I reached in my bag to grab a cleaning cloth - I wiped the blood that was dripping all around it. I then took a needle and thread out my bag and ...

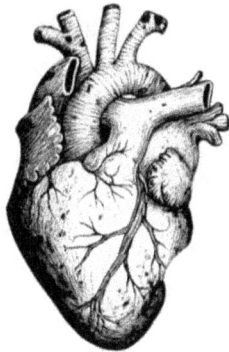

"You want to look back, but you don't want to go back - know the difference."

You have to learn how to separate the feelings of missing someone from the act of going back into a situation that may not be best for your life. Every feeling doesn't necessarily need to be acted upon. Missing someone goes away once enough time is spent without them. So make sure the situation is right and not just right for right now.

"People who can't commit to one person are like drivers who can't commit to one lane on a crowded interstate. Sooner or later, there's going to be an accident."

It's just a matter of time before a collision takes place. Hopefully it's nothing fatal, but instead fixable. Sometimes you have to close your lane so they can't swerve back in yours.

"There's a difference between giving up on a relationship and ending it because your partner isn't trying to make it work; their actions should show effort."

Women often tell me how they don't want to give up on their relationship. I give them credit for their fight. But where does the line get drawn? Is there a thin line between being a fighter and being foolish? Abusive relationships, men who make drastic changes in character, habitual cheaters; how many passes do they get? How long do you fight for someone who isn't fighting for you? There isn't an exact answer, for we all have our own individual limits. But I must tell you, when your options are *"give up on my relationship"* or *"give up on my happiness,"* it's probably time to make some changes.

ASK DR. LINQ

"You being single may just mean that you're so unique that it's not easy to find a match for you."

You can find parts for a Toyota up the street, but for a Bentley you might have to wait on those. Embrace your patience and love yourself regardless of where the chips fall. There's no need to rush your situation. Everyone's happiness comes at different times.

ASK DR. LINQ

"I never stopped caring - I just choose to care for me more now."

Sometimes people will push you to the point where they almost force you to choose between them and you. Life would be so much easier if you didn't have to. But when you're faced with that difficult decision, do what happiness tells you. Happiness is the best road to love, whether it's with them or not.

"You only go backwards when you're afraid of what's ahead."

Are you afraid of what life has waiting for you up ahead? How about you tell life what you're going to do instead. Don't be the result of, be the cause of. Be the reason why things happen instead of just watching things happen. When we lose certain people, it can be scary to imagine life without them. The unknown can be very scary; first times can be scary as well. But remember that fear doesn't exist, it's not a real thing. In this case, it's doubts and all the other negative thoughts your mind can conjure up, transformed into an unpleasant emotion. Understand that you can move forward and slowly create your world to the best of your ability. Your fears are fairy tales.

"Don't have me standing in line waiting for a ride that hasn't been built yet."

Last thing you want is to have someone convince you that you two will be together only to drag you along to a place of nothing. In some cases they may continue to have you stand in line for as long as you choose to stay. Yes, **choose**... surprise! Sometimes we wait for someone so long we forget what we're waiting for. When they remind us, we no longer want it.

"Occasionally the best gifts are given when you're not looking."

Sometimes we look for something for so long and never find it. The moment we stop looking and focus on ourselves, it shows up. This happens with love, your cigarette lighter, the time clock at work, etc. Relax; your hunt may be the flaw. That may be the reason it seems like it's taking so long to show up. When you watch the clock at work, waiting for 5 o'clock, it ticks the slowest, or so it seems.

"Make sure they are willing to do the same things that you would do for them."

They may show their true colors when they have to start putting in some effort. The best way to see if someone is a failure is to test them. If you don't allow their dedication to be tested, you'll never know what you have. You can't be afraid to scare people away. They should be embarrassed, not you. Ask direct questions and you should expect direct answers.

ASK DR. LINQ

"I had to stop watering dead grass. I'm the only one paying the water bill around here."

When you're the only one that's trying to make it last, it comes to a point where you have to turn the water hose off and let it die. Especially if your partner is just standing there flicking lit cigarettes on the lawn. What happens when your money is all spent and you can't afford the bill? It dies anyway, but now it's dead and you're broke. Just like in a relationship, what happens when you stay in it even though you both know it's over? Your time is spent and it dies anyway.

ASK DR. LINQ

"The problem isn't with the goals we set. The problem is with our habits that contradict these goals."

It takes a lifestyle change to accomplish your goals. You have to really be about this change. Setting the goal is the easy part; resetting your mind is when it gets tricky. Make sure your everyday activities are aligned with what you want to accomplish. You have the same amount of hours in a day as any celebrity has; they just use theirs better than you.

"Sometimes you have to break the news to your heart that it's over. What makes it hard is when your heart doesn't believe you."

Often the mind goes downstairs to have a word with your heart and give it an update. The heart may reject it or accept it depending on how much control you have given it. Sometimes the heart will yell so loudly at the mind that it will send the mind back upstairs with its tail between its legs. Who's the head of your control center? Hopefully you have a good balance of following your mind and following your heart until it's about to lead you off a cliff.

"He can have all the candy in the world - he's still going to want a real meal."

Having more than good looks can get a man, but it doesn't guarantee that you and he will stay together. You can be the best woman on earth; if he isn't ready, it probably will not work. With all that being said, it still helps to have more than less. These eye candy women he may be dealing with now will never be as fulfilling as soul food. You can't live off candy forever.

"We can't just say we're Kings and Queens - we have to act like it as well."

We are living right now; no past or future time is here with us, just things from the past and thoughts of the future. Now is the time to become what you claim you are. Even if you don't see it on the outside of you, see it on the inside. Tell yourself what you are and don't let the world tell you any different. Then walk in the footsteps of it and watch it manifest in the physical. It takes effort; chip at it daily.

"When the present is going bad, it can make the past look appealing again. Be careful, it's more than likely just a mirage."

I've seen a lot of women come to the conclusion that since dating the new guy didn't work out, it automatically means that the old guy is the only fit. That's not always true. Is this perceived failure with the new guy discouraging? Yes, but it doesn't mean that the last guy is the only person you will mesh well with. You'll never know what's next until you continue to move forward.

<u>The Surgery</u>

....I put some stitches across the gaping hole. The blood started flowing out again as it began to rapidly beat - signifying that it was giving all it had for one last attempt to stay alive...

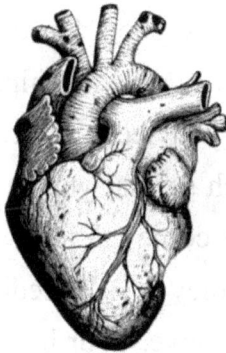

"Just because something makes you feel good, doesn't mean it is good. This alone lets us know that our feelings can lead us astray."

Have you ever bitten into something and felt this deep warm feeling of pleasure? I think we all have. Food can make us feel great for a short period of time. Our subconscious mind remembers that great feeling and wants more of it, dopamine. But not all great tasting food is good for us; it's a somewhat similar scenario with relationships. Sometimes that person can make you feel that awesome temporary happiness, so much so that you're blinded by what's ahead. You may become addicted to the sweet taste, not realizing that they aren't feeding you the proper love minerals to survive. Your heart starts to rot from the inside out and the relationship dies a cold death. So make sure you *love healthy!*

"A relationship should be more of a partnership than a dictatorship."

You shouldn't feel like a prisoner in your relationship. You may think that's a sign of him being a strong man, but it might be a sign of how insecure he is inside. When trust issues can't be controlled properly, they can cause people to act like prison guards of your house. In today's world the responsibilities of the household are pretty much even, and I think that's fair.

"Every night I want to have an affair with the person I married."

When your life partner is also your person on the side, it can be beautiful. If you're going to cheat on me, cheat on me with me. I believe switching things up in the bedroom is important. It doesn't guarantee a non-cheating relationship, but it may bring some excitement back to a place that was once without a pulse. *Let's role play!*

ASK DR. LINQ

"You can tell the type of person you were dealing with once you no longer have a relationship with them. Would they slander your name - or move on?"

Some people have that evil in them; they just need you to make them mad enough for it to show. The scary part is that sometimes they don't even realize it's inside them. You get out of a relationship and they try to date your enemy or someone close to you just to get a reaction. Understand that their actions come from something going on within them, so try not to take it personal. They want to hurt you, but they can't reach what they no longer have access to. In the end, they're only hurting themselves.

"If I tell you what I don't like, and I continue to go through it, you must not like me enough, if you continue to do it."

You tell them it hurts and they don't stop. What could possibly be the reason? Probably a lack of emotion or a lack of love for you. Either way, you should be catering to their needs and they should cater to yours. If this dynamic is going only one way, changes should be made accordingly.

"I forgive you - but it will never be the same."

You don't laugh at their jokes as loud, you don't crave their touch anymore because your mind keeps replaying the times they cheated on you. Your heart has gone cold toward them. Sometimes the damage is too deep to repair. The insurance company won't pay for the fix. It might be time for a new car.

"If you're moving in a positive direction, how can you lose someone and consider it a bad thing? It may be a part of the positive journey."

When you're traveling on your path and you know that your goal is within reach, the loss of someone off your path was more than likely for good reason. When I say lose, I don't mean by death, I mean by circumstances. When it doesn't work out, it's probably because they didn't fit your positive path. And that's okay.

"You make it hard for me to love you; I'll make it hard for you to find me."

Sometimes you have to separate yourself from someone who purposely does things that make it almost impossible to share your love with them. The more you stick around, the greater the chances they will push you over the edge. So if they don't feel the need to live in harmony with you, don't live with them, period. Harsh way to look at it, I know, but what do you do when someone continues to give you their ass to kiss? Keep kissing or get going?

"Calm down; they don't hate you or what you're doing. They hate themselves because they couldn't do it."

Don't worry, it may just be something they're dealing with inside. You may be the key that opens the door for the release of their actions. It may be easier said than done, but don't take it too personal. We can't allow the evils of others to find their way into our life by even mentioning them. Once you mention it, it becomes a part of your mental. Their hate isn't worth that much.

"You can wish for their change all you want, if they don't want to - it means nothing."

Even if the change is beneficial to them, if they don't see it that way, they won't change. Sometimes the most we can do is ask, suggest, and offer. Once we do that, if we don't like what we see in them, we may need to change our view - maybe a view without them in it.

"Nothing is more annoying than a person that acts as though they brought everything to the table - when they're the reason the table has only 3 legs!"

Have you ever had someone treat you as if you wouldn't be anything without them? Talk to you like they're the reason you have what you have, when in reality they're the reason you don't have as much as you should. These people are semi-delusional, but they can't help it. They see the world through selfish eyes. They only see their good; they can't see their bad.

ASK DR. LINQ

"Your qualifications for a good man should scare some guys away. If they don't, maybe they aren't high enough."

Everyone can't be accepted, can they? They shouldn't. When you set your standards high, guys who want to get to know you will jump to reach them. Most guys probably will not, depending on how high you set them. So yes, you will scare some men away. But that's all a part of the weeding out process. Set the rules in the beginning. If you don't, he may never know where he stands or what you expect from him. If you wait, then you finally do tell him, he may not like your expectations. Which is fine, but if you've grown a strong attachment to him it could make things complicated.

"The problem is people are getting into relationships when deep down inside they know they're not ready."

You can't force emotions and expect them to be genuine. Natural feeling comes in natural timing. Some guys do this out of fear of losing the female they're dealing with, or he knows she wants a relationship so he does it to make her happy, or he's using her for some situational gain like a place to stay, etc. Regardless of the reasoning why, it normally always ends badly. You take a bite before he's done cooking and you may get sick.

"Some say when you reach the top, down is the only place to go. I say that's when you start to fly."

How do you view life? Are you missing out on opportunities because you view the world in a negative way? That will probably lead to a negative life. There are a lot of people who want to see good people lose. Maybe they should change their view. The view from the top is beautiful, but the sky is the limit. Take your best to the top and when you get there, take it across the world.

"Don't weigh your life on someone else's scale."

Someone else's key to happiness doesn't always fit your lock. Be cautious of the temptation to compare your life with someone else's, especially if you find that comparison bringing you down. Their happiness comes along with its own built-in sadness; always remember that.

The Recovery

....Then the beating slowed and it stabilized at a normal rate. I smiled because I knew I had made a difference – I knew that I had helped in the healing process of this beautiful creation from its hopeless state of being. Then a towering woman I'd never met before entered the room...

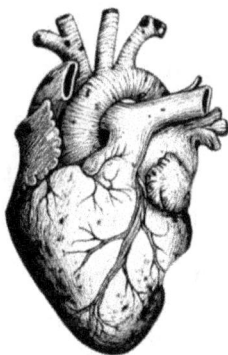

"Next time you might want to pick your fruit from higher up on the tree. Those aren't for everyone."

Make sure the guys you pick from aren't the guys everyone has already had a bite of unless you want the same results. Choose a better quality of man and you increase your chances of receiving a better quality relationship. Usually, better quality men are at better quality events. Recognize the type of guy you have. If you have a party guy (and you dislike parties) expect him to still want to party. I know… you would like to think that once he gets in a relationship he should change his ways. Most don't. Some do though, and some do at first and later grow resentment towards her. That's when he starts to feel like she's trying to change him when in fact he should be compromising. But since you can't control his ultimate decisions, you may be better off choosing the guy you want from the beginning instead of picking the science project you want to mold.

"There's a difference between being lonely and being alone."

A simple Google search would back up this statement. But I want to make it clear that if you find peace and happiness within, being alone doesn't have to lead to being lonely. When you make a choice of choosing to be alone rather than to be disrespected, there's nothing wrong with that. The problem really comes in when you feel that your happiness has to be made by someone else. Can someone come along and introduce you to new things and brighten your life up? Absolutely. Living a life that doesn't have purpose unless someone else is in it can be beautiful when you have them; it can also be very dangerous when you don't. I believe in personal love for life, positive vibrations brought to someone else's positive vibration to create a special relationship. When you're living a life that allows you to have fun while you accomplish your goals, you never spend a day feeling lonely even when you are alone.

"Life before them was good; it'll be good after them as well."

Sometimes we become so attached to people who enter our lives that we forget how life was before they arrived. Sometimes we become so dependent on them that we forget how to function without them. I can tell you now, your life may have improved with them in it, but before they came along you were alive. You were living; you found a way to make it. That person is still in you. Never forget that.

"Their perfect relationship may function different than yours. Yours has to fit your life."

This is why I like to ask, *"Are you happy?"* Because that's what it boils down to, are you both happy? If so, then your relationship is in a good state regardless of how others may be progressing. The problem approaches when you start to compare your relationship with someone else's. We tend to use everyone else's life as a point of reference concerning our own. But remember, their happiness comes along with its own sadness, doubts, and frustrations.

"I want someone who can find someone better than me; but still chooses me."

Isn't that what the majority of us expect, someone who can see something in us that others cannot? Just knowing that you have someone who could probably find a better looking person or a more financially secure person, yet still chooses you, means a lot. It should also inspire you to become the person your significant other deserves if you feel you're not at your best in life. Not only will that make them want you even more, but you'll be improving yourself in the process.

"If they tell you they don't love you, believe them; they're not confused. If so, they believe it's true anyway - So they're going to act according to their belief."

Believe them even if their actions indicate otherwise at times. You don't want to misjudge the situation, and when they finally show you that they don't love you, you forget that they already gave you a heads-up. They tell you they **don't** love you - listen to their words. They tell you they **do** love you - watch their actions.

"The grass doesn't have to be greener on the other side - I'm the fertilizer!"

Some people have developed the gift of making everything they touch seem better. Every situation they are dropped in, they improve it. These are people who are living and breathing growth in the flesh. They get a high from watching things improve from their touch. I believe we all should have that mindset. We should all walk into new situations with the intention of making them better.

ASK DR. LINQ

"Place your significant other on high ground. That way the average person walking by can't reach them."

When you treat the one you love so special, it brings value to your friendship. In turn, it makes it hard for them to even think about being taken away from you. When you raise them up, you are also raising the value of **you** in their life. But when that value is low, anyone can match your price and buy them off your hands.

ASK DR. LINQ

"Life doesn't end after your last relationship. It either gets better or worse - but that depends on your next move."

When it's all said and done, what happens next? Luckily, you have the opportunity to make life better than it once was and to turn a negative situation into something positive. As I've stated before, the best revenge is to improve your life. People can become our habits, so in order to move on from them, we have to replace one habit with another, preferably a habit that will help you reach a lifelong goal. The time you would normally spend with them can now be turned into time accomplishing something meaningful for yourself. We all have 24 hours in a day. That time will be spent one way or another, so make it work for you instead of working against you.

"As human beings we long for connection to other like beings. But the more you try to be relatable to everyone, the more you're relatable to no one."

It's natural for us to want that human connection and to never feel that we are the only ones going through this thing called life. But sometimes we try so hard to connect to everyone and please as many people as we can, we begin to act out of character; we lose who we are. It also makes us seem confused and complicated, which in turn makes us less connectable to others. The best way to solve this problem is to make sure we are ourselves and not just putting on fake personas to please everyone. You are special, and your unique self will be what attracts people to you.

"We have to start viewing ourselves as worthy. Worthy to be treated a certain way; worthy of a certain profession and not victims of circumstance."

Every celebrity that you look at has the same amount of hours in a day as you do. What are you doing with your time? What and who are you letting dictate your life? You have every right to be treated the way you want. But you have to understand that in order to be treated a certain way by someone, you have to show that you deserve it. But first and most importantly, know it within yourself; that's where it starts. After that, it will manifest externally on its own. Be great now and great responsibility will come to lead you to great success. So become what you want and don't wait for it to happen. It's not going to unless you make a conscious effort to turn it into a reality.

"The alligator crawled out the water, to find some food on land - he left his home, dry ground he roamed, when he returned his lake was sand."

You can't allow people to come and go as they please. If you do, they have no reason to please you. If home is always available when they mess up, there's no need to care for home; it's not going anywhere. Also, if you're on the other side of the situation, make sure you keep your eyes on what is important. You look away, and it may be gone when you look back.

"Once you add value to your life, you only settle when someone proves to be worthy enough to be a part of it."

The world revolves around the idea of value. People view people in this way as well. You have to ask yourself, "What do I bring to the table?" Is it something that's unique? The unfortunate part is that sometimes people view **value** in different ways, so they may not recognize yours. It's not that they can't see your worth necessarily; it's just that worth to them is something different. This is why really getting to know someone in the beginning of a relationship is very important. A simple conversation could solve that mystery. If they value something you don't offer, they may not be the one for you.

"Some people come in your life to help, some come to hurt - which one are they?"

It's beautiful when you can step back and examine the people who are around you. I believe it's always important to evaluate the ones you spend your time with. You may be hurting or experiencing some setbacks and don't know why, you may find it in them.

"We have to give <u>and</u> take. One sided situations aren't healthy. Sometimes good givers make the mistake of never taking - you have to do both."

You have to be able to take and they have to be able to give. If what they're giving you is junk, the body and spirit may reject it, but the mind will soak it in. This will cause you discomfort and throw off your alignment. So yes, give good and make sure you take good. If they have nothing good to give, things may begin to fall apart. Sometimes we're so used to giving, we don't expect to receive; it's always good to receive. Why? One reason is because the person you are receiving from may need to give. You may just be their outlet. This world is based on balance; be balanced.

The Realization

...She stared at me then glanced down at the heart which was in my hand. She then grabbed her chest and realized there was a black hole where she once generated love. I reached out and handed her the heart; she smiled and took hold of it. "What is your name?" I asked. She said...

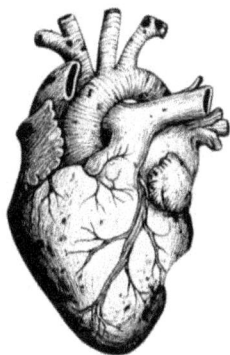

"You have the key that unlocks your happiness within."

One thing we can control is ourselves. We lose control at times, but that's only because we allow it. Happiness isn't in a car, house, or even a person. Those things are merely vessels to allow our own inner happiness to express itself. Being able to tap into that inner happiness takes a lot of cutting away. What I mean is you have to cut away all of that negative garbage you continue to drag along with you on your journey. You have people you continue to interact with that are nothing but negative clouds. You participate in activities that bring you no satisfaction after they are done. You watch shows that showcase other people's problems, which incites negative emotions inside you. You eat foods that keep you sluggish and unenthusiastic. Cut those away! Watch what you put inside your body, mind, and spirit. You have the key hidden inside... find it.

"The plan ahead is far greater than the problems behind."

How can words so simple mean so much? Those who succeed live in the future. Those who fail live in the past. Sometimes we let the ills of yesteryear become the blueprint of tomorrow, when in fact those ills should only be the outline of what not to do, not the outline of what will happen. I strongly believe in aligning your thoughts with what you want and not with what you have. Let's say you truly don't want to fail. Do not think or say, "I don't want to fail!" Instead think or say, "I will succeed!" This is how to think positive and how you align yourself with what you want and ignore that which you do not. Only speak adding words when making commands upon your life and do not mention subtracting words.

ASK DR.LINQ

"I care way too much for people who don't deserve it. One day I'll run out of cares to give."

Often we find ourselves spending our valuable time and energy on things that give us nothing in return. Often these things are people. It becomes a problem when we begin doing less for those who actually deserve our care. Caring for the less deserving can cause frustration because of their lack of returning care. This may cause us to lash out or become reluctant to give to others in fear that they too will take our kindness for granted. Always remember the give and take philosophy.

"Sometimes progressing in life can scare you away and make you want to stay where you are. Don't fall for that trap, being scared can mean something good."

There's going to be a lot of situations you face in life that do not make sense to you; situations that you can't seem to understand the root of, situations that you can't seem to figure out how to solve yet. The key word is yet. In order for you to grow, you often have to face things you've never faced before, good and bad. Don't let it get you down, we all face them and are just as lost as you. You are a seed and in order for a seed to grow through the dirt it was planted in, it has to pass new soil, soil it has never seen. The unknown can be scary, but just know you're growing through it and sooner or later it will become your norm until your next journey.

"What you have as of now is exactly what you want and what you feel you should have at <u>this point</u> in life - according to the uncontrollable setbacks you've faced."

We have choices, some choices harder than others; but they are our options nonetheless. I'm not a big fan of solely placing blame on others for where I am in life. I believe taking responsibility for what I have and where I am is the first step in fixing it. So if someone screws me over, I recognize their obvious actions but I also take full blame for choosing to deal with them. By doing this I shed light on my decision making skills and can make necessary changes if needed. There are situations that we have no control over that hinder our progression and make our choices hard. But we still have the power to tackle all dreams that are possible. If we don't tackle them, we don't want them bad enough. So what we have is what we want, our efforts speak louder than our words.

ASK DR. LINQ

"Don't become jealous over things you had the opportunity to have but never chose to."

When you don't take advantage of opportunities, you have to accept the fact that you missed the chance. When you have someone special and did things that ran them off to someone else, you have to accept the fact that you missed the opportunity. It's not always a bad thing to lose something; it's often just the result of who you are. Things that are to be a part of your life will normally find a way to be; things that are not will not. But what we can't do is become vengeful, envious, and jealous of what we once had or had the opportunity to have. Instead, let us recognize that it may not have been for us, and that's perfectly okay. This may be your learning lesson.

"If your partner doesn't have a plan for the future, which direction are you two building?"

We have to stop living day to day until we die, we really do. Ten years will be here before you know it, and you're going to wish you had made some calculated steps this day, week, or month toward your future. If you have but your significant other hasn't, communicate the importance of it with them today. Don't talk down on them, but ask a few questions about the future. I don't know if anything brings a couple together mentally more than creating ideas does. If this is the person you want to share your future with, sit down and draw up the blueprint with them. Creation is love, ask the energy above.

"Successful people are no different than you. There is a lane for you to conquer."

Only difference between you and successful people is that **they decided** to be successful and **you want** to be successful. It's not solely talent, luck, nor financial advantage. People from all walks of life become successful regardless of race, nationality, or social class. The fact remains that one day they all said, "Enough is enough!" They used their time wisely, something you haven't been able to do. They realized that every piece of entertainment that isn't created by them is a potential roadblock. They stopped watching other successful people live their dreams and started living their own. They figured out that the only reason they should watch other successful people is for learning purposes to further their own growth, not to feed their entertainment addiction.

"If you don't set the standards, they will make their own."

If you don't let them know exactly where you stand, they will put you where they feel you should be standing. Some women are afraid to have a strong stance when dealing with men. These women are normally women who are afraid to run men off. So they leave the playing field open instead of making the guidelines clear. Women who have strong stances and inform men of their stances are normally women who are not afraid of running a man away. They aren't to the point where they want any guy; they want a guy that fits them. She understands that if he doesn't talk to her because of how she feels, he obviously isn't for her. You cannot lose by letting them know what is and isn't acceptable early in the dating stage.

"It takes 7 seconds to text me."

In today's world we celebrate the fact that we can communicate with each other faster than ever. With that comes the pressure of quick responses. So those excuses you have about why you couldn't communicate with me today mean nothing to me. If they can't dedicate 7 seconds out of their day to you, what's the point? But on the other side of the coin, is 7 seconds worth any value anyway? Should we even view texting as something that is valuable, being that it takes such a short time to send and doesn't require much effort? If it has no true value, could we really be mad at their non-responsive ways? Don't let your mobile device make you a lazy lover. Don't think that your text messages are substitutes for your relationship actions. Texting is only a substitute for phone conversations.

"Sometimes you have to jump out in the water to realize it's actually not deep - you just might enjoy it."

If you truly feel it is right and have weighed all options, go for it. After the fear of the leap is gone, you'll be glad you did. You have one life to live, so don't spend another minute in a situation you aren't happy with. Too many people talk their way back into staying in places they don't want to be in. Don't be that person trying to justify the wrongs of your circumstances.

"Sometimes there is that one person you keep a bond with for a long time."

It's weird how those close friends you've never been in a relationship with seem to never go away. It's also weird how you can't leave them alone sometimes. Time spent with them seems perfect. But remember, time with them may be deluded. It's one thing to be great friends for 5+ years. It's another to be in a relationship for 5+ years. Arguments, concerns and expectations of your significant other are normally not present with this good close friend. Things may be different if you two became one. Right now it may be good with them because there are no real expectations, but once commitment is added to the equation, that often changes things.

"I can tell you where you're going to be tomorrow by looking at your habits today."

You're living life with no end in sight, you will fail. You know why? You're waiting to see what happens next instead of making something happen next. You keep telling yourself that you'll start next week, you don't. You tell yourself, "Something's got to give," it doesn't. Nothing is coming to save you. Get up and work for it or stay average. That's it. The next five years will come and you will be saying the exact same thing you're saying today. Do you realize that? Think five years back, thought you'd be further by now, huh? The everyday habits you have today will determine the goals you tackle tomorrow.

"When all you know is getting hurt, it's hard to walk away from what you're comfortable with."

Most of us want change, but hate making changes to achieve that change; in some cases even if our current state is one that hurts us. Fear of what's next for us is so frightening at times that we will actually choose to stay in situations that are not healthy for us. But because these current situations are familiar, we identify them as being good enough, but they aren't. Once you realize that you create your future, you eliminate the initial fear aspect and you are able to move away from any situation that may cause you pain.

ASK DR. LINQ

"Sometimes no response is the best response."

It's well known that communication is essential in having a healthy relationship. But sometimes not promptly responding to anger-invoking statements can save you from unnecessary arguments. Give yourself some time to calm down and respond later, not just in relationships but in life in general. Responding to random people who piss you off but hold no weight in your life is frankly just a waste of time. The best way to end an argument with them is to stop talking. They want you to understand their point just as much as you want them to understand yours. You can show them that their point means absolutely nothing to you by not responding. I guess silence can be golden.

The Understanding

..."My name is not important just yet. What is important is that you share your words with all my children." She placed the heart in her chest and took a deep breath. "Your children?" I asked. "Where would I find them?" She looked down at me, all covered in blood and said, "They are where you are, they live where you live, they see what you see and they give what you give – they are you and you are them. And me...I'm Mother Earth – child to only the greatest energy above....

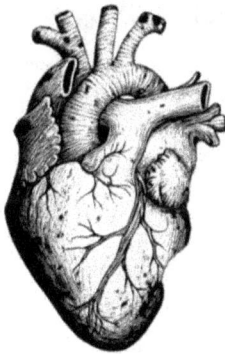

"Time has a PhD in healing. It's the greatest doctor on earth."

Sometimes we have to let time take hold of certain situations when we're in stages of pain, especially when dealing with relationship hurt. The most important thing is that during this period, you are building yourself to be stronger than you once were. Use this painful moment as a catapult to send you to the next level of excellence. Don't view this stage as a setback, but as a setup. Dr. Time is going to accompany you along this journey. So laugh and have some good conversations with him; he's awesome if you treat him special.

"Become who you want to spend the rest of your life with."

Millions of people wouldn't marry themselves if they had the chance to. They may think that they would, but they wouldn't. You don't see the complaints you dish out every day, the negative mindset you live with, the doubts you present to yourself regularly, and the excuses you give as to why things aren't the way they should be. The only way to attract positive people is to be what you're trying to attract. Good vibes move in harmony with one another. Think positive, eat positive, and stay in positive surroundings. Negative people are never really there.

"Sometimes you have to stop loving and start living."

Love can blind you so much, you can lose track of what's right and of what's best for you in order to have a healthy life. So sometimes it's best to cut certain loves off. True love is one with positive life, so you can't detach from that. But when your love for something or even someone is actually causing a hindrance to your life, or if it's keeping you from being you, it's time to separate yourself.

"You can't control what has happened, but you can control what happens next. Now is the time to start being proactive and not reactive."

I know it's common sense, but sometimes it seems we forget that what has happened is gone. The effects of it may linger on, but you have the power to make a decision today on how you handle it. Some things may be harder to decide on, especially if a particular train of thought is deeply embedded in the subconscious mind. But it starts with a final decision, then a positive attitude in general, and then a true belief behind whatever you want to add to the subconscious mind. We have to find as much joy as possible in today's events. Right now you have a choice to view your life as half full or half empty. Make a choice to be happy by all means.

ASK DR. LINQ

"Ladies, you can't run around feeling fulfilled that 100's of guys want to sleep with you."

A greater goal is to have hundreds of guys who want to be in a relationship with you. You may find it better to have one guy who finds your mind attractive than to have one hundred guys who find your body attractive. Nothing wrong with being desired by people. Nothing wrong with being sexually desired by multiple people. The problem ensues when you confuse sexual desire with someone actually liking you and desiring to learn more about you. We see individuals who brag about how many guys want to sleep with them, as if that's a goal. Now, if that is in fact your goal to sleep with multiple men or to use your body as a way to provide a living of some sort, pay this no mind. Often women can see tons of guys trying to talk to them and then get confused as to why their relationships don't work. We can't mistake people who are trying to get to know the inner you with people who have merely met the outer you and are only concerned with that.

"Never stand next to a King if you have to play his servant and not his Queen. He may be a servant in disguise."

If your position is to be on his side, there is no reason why you should be standing under him. A relationship is a business that you both own, co-owners and co-founders. Imagine him treating you as an employee. Imagine him treating you like an extra in the cinematic movie of your relationship. It wouldn't make sense to stick around for that when you're the star as well. Always know your position and expect to be treated as such. Don't you think you deserve it? If he's treating you as a "servant," it may be because he is one as well and that's how he lives. So it's only natural that he treats you the same way.

"Feeling sorry isn't feeling change."

Just because they realized they messed up doesn't mean they have changed. Learning your lesson does not mean you've implemented the new lesson. Make sure they follow through with the apology. An apology isn't just the words "I apologize." It's the actions that follow the words that make the apology come full circle.

"We can't move forward until we see the same path."

When a couple becomes one, there can't be any forward progress until they both learn how to agree on important issues. We all come from different walks of life and so do our opinions of the world. Many people get into relationships for reasons that have nothing to do with visions of the future. As a result, many couples later find that the person they were happy with just sharing good times is not on the same page as them concerning their future lives. Always make sure that their vision is aligned with yours before you let your heart lead the way. Once you commit to someone, you're committing your life to them. Your decisions are not only yours for the most part. So if you two can't come to an agreement on east or west, that car may just sit there until then. Sometimes we have to trust our partner's leadership decisions though. But only after they have proven to be leader-worthy. I'm hoping that you've evaluated them before the relationship started to know whether or not they are good at decision making. That's more important than what their favorite color is.

"Some look at the road ahead and see a lonely walk going nowhere. I look and see a peaceful drive to my destination."

The beauty is in the eye of the beholder. Always remember to find the joy, it will benefit you. The negative will not, so why look for it? When it comes at you without want, ignore it, your words give it life. Find the good in the journey and stay away from the bad. Every road has some beauty on it. You just have to be in a beautiful state of mind to see it.

"You won't be hurt forever. The pains of right now do not exist in the future."

There's going to come a time when you are going to feel just fine. Right now you may feel empty. We attach to people and things almost like sticking a plug into an outlet. Once that connection is abruptly disconnected, there's a void. You may be feeling the void right now. We miss that energy that was once flowing through us. Now is the time to work on you. Setting new goals is a great way to get over something. The more you focus on you, the less you can focus on them or any other outside love. Time to use your inner love and share it with the world. Practice spreading your happiness; we often find ourselves when we're trying to help others...I did.

<u>The Revelation</u>

..."Understood," I said. We then hugged each other and she thanked me for helping her find herself. She turned around and left out the same way in which she had come. As she was walking away I felt an instant pain. I looked down and I realized I had a black hole in my chest where my heart once was – I had given my heart to her. At that moment I truly understood my purpose. Give my all to the world – my truths, my beliefs and my love. You never know who may need it. Who am I kidding...we all need it.

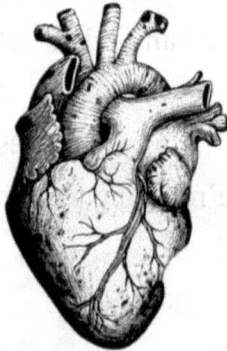

Thank you for reading, I can't say that enough.

I truly want to say you are loved, regardless of what you see on TV, what you read in the paper, or what people show you on social media. There are some good people in this world. People who want to make sure that when they leave this planet, they leave it a little better than it once was before they got here. You may be like me, searching for meaning and purpose in life, I can't say. But what I believe is that we are all here to experience the beauty of life. All its ups and downs and all its pleasures and pains. Embrace those moments when you cry alone in your room; we all have them. We all cry alone at some point in life, it's a part of the ride. The biggest myth is that you and I are not connected, we are. We both share the same emotions; we laugh hard and cry hard. We have to try our best to be our best and to love the simple fact that we can breathe another day. Make this day count for something.

If no one else loves you, I do.

Sincerely Yours, Me.

THE AGREEMENT

By signing on the line below, I promise to spend every day looking for a moment to laugh. I will no longer view my life as something that happens to me, but something I make happen. I agree that I am in control of what I was sent here to do and I will find and fulfill my mission. I will no longer stay in any situation that may slow my growth or cause me sorrow. I promise that from this day forth I will watch what goes inside my body and my mind. I will choose education over entertainment. I will make everyone around me better, and I will love my life regardless of my many flaws.

I will....be happy.

Signed, _____

Only if you mean it.